THE
HUMAN SIDE
OF DEADLINES
A PROJECT MANAGER'S DIARY

ARCHANA SHANKAR

BLUEROSE PUBLISHERS
India | U.K.

Copyright © Archana Shankar 2025

All rights reserved by author. No part of this publication may be reproduced, stored in a retrieval system or transmitted in any form or by any means, electronic, mechanical, photocopying, recording or otherwise, without the prior permission of the author. Although every precaution has been taken to verify the accuracy of the information contained herein, the publisher assumes no responsibility for any errors or omissions. No liability is assumed for damages that may result from the use of information contained within.

BlueRose Publishers takes no responsibility for any damages, losses, or liabilities that may arise from the use or misuse of the information, products, or services provided in this publication.

For permissions requests or inquiries regarding this publication, please contact:

BLUEROSE PUBLISHERS
www.BlueRoseONE.com
info@bluerosepublishers.com
+91 8882 898 898
+4407342408967

ISBN: 978-93-6783-800-6

Cover Design: Shubham Verma
Typesetting: Sagar

First Edition: March 2025

This book is lovingly dedicated to my Nani Maa (Matangi Jha), who took her last breath on July 5, 2024. Her love and wisdom continue to inspire me every day. I also sincerely dedicate this book to my Nana Jee, Shri B.K. Jha, whose guidance and values have shaped my journey. With deep respect and gratitude, I extend this dedication to my paternal grandparents and to my beloved village, Sarisab—a place that holds countless memories and the roots of my story.

I wholeheartedly dedicate this book to my loving parents (Maa- Smt. Abha Jha & Dada- Shri Binod Shankar Jha),whose unwavering support and blessings have been my greatest strength. With equal gratitude, I extend this dedication to my in-laws (Maa- Smt. Dhurpati Singh & Papa- Shri R.K. Singh), whose kindness and encouragement have always been a source of inspiration.

Acknowledgment: Why I Chose This Topic

Every project manager has stories—some triumphant, some chaotic, and some downright hilarious. Over the course of my 18-year career, I have lived these stories, learning not just about deadlines and deliverables but about the people who make them happen. I chose to write this book because I believe there is an untold human side to project management—an intricate dance of emotions, relationships, and resilience that goes beyond spreadsheets and status updates.

This book is a celebration of those who thrive under pressure, who juggle expectations with empathy, and who find humour even in the midst of chaos. It is for every manager who has ever dealt with impossible clients, tight deadlines, and unpredictable team dynamics, yet found a way to deliver—because that's what we do.

On a personal note, I was inspired by the many roles I play in life: a professional balancing work challenges, a mother raising two amazing sons, a wife navigating a partnership in the same field, and the youngest member of a large, loving family. My experiences taught me that managing a team is not unlike managing a family—both require patience, adaptability, and a healthy dose of humour.

Through this book, I hope to share the lessons, laughter, and moments of clarity that have shaped my journey, with the hope that readers—whether project managers, aspiring leaders, or just curious minds—find inspiration, guidance, and a sense of camaraderie.

This is my way of honouring the people, experiences, and stories that have taught me to see the bigger picture, even when the smallest task seemed overwhelming. Thank you for being part of this journey with me.

About the Author

Archana is a dynamic and passionate computer engineer with over 18 years of experience in the IT industry, specializing in QA, project management, and change coordination. Known for her knack for solving complex problems and juggling multiple projects, she often jokes that her multitasking skills were perfected not in the boardroom but in her bustling home.

Outside of work, she is a proud mother to two remarkable sons: her elder son (Akshat), a diligent boarding school student aiming to exceed expectations in academics, and her younger son (Agastya), a rising chess prodigy and badminton enthusiast who recently claimed first place in his debut chess competition.

Married to a fellow computer engineer, Archana thrives in a household where debates on algorithms and coffee brewing methods are equally intense. A special thank you to him (Dharmendra Singh), whose unwavering support, love, and encouragement have been my greatest source of strength. Your belief in me and my dreams has made this journey possible, and for that, I am forever grateful.

I am deeply grateful to my parents, Abha Jha and Prof. B.S. Jha, whose unwavering support, values, and inspiration have shaped the person I am today. Their guidance and love have been my foundation. I also extend heartfelt thanks to my in-laws, Maa and Papa Jee, for their encouragement and belief in me. Their blessings have always been my strength.

As the youngest member of her in-laws' family, she has mastered the art of blending humour, humility, and wisdom, which makes her a beloved maasi, chachi, and mami to all energetic nieces and nephews (Priyanka, Shivangi, Priti, Kamini, Rajani, Roshni, Mayank, Alok, Aditya, Naman, Ansh, Abhinav and Laado)—transforming every family gathering into a mini festival.

Growing up with the joy and camaraderie of two sisters (Shalu and Priyam) and one brother (Rishi), she cherishes the lifelong bond of siblinghood, which continues to be her source of strength. Her extended family includes 5 wonderful sisters-in-law (Guddi Singh, Usha Singh, Babita singh & Sandeepta) and 4 brother in-law (Yogendra Singh, Chandrasen Singh, Nandan Jha & Chandan Jha) ensuring that life is filled with warmth, laughter, and plenty of good-natured teasing.

Last but not least, my heartfelt thanks to my organization, my incredible colleagues, and dear friends, who serve as my daily source of strength and motivation. Your support and camaraderie have been invaluable in this journey.

Through her writing, Archana aspires to share her journey of balancing career, family, and the delightful chaos of life. Whether managing deadlines, raising future leaders, or navigating the dynamics of a big family, she believes there is always room for a hearty laugh and a good story. Her debut book promises to bring readers a mix of wisdom, humour, and heartfelt anecdotes that resonate across all walks of life.

Disclaimer
A Personal Journey in Project Management

This book is not intended to be a comprehensive guide or definitive source of all the certifications and learning you should pursue to enhance your project management skills. Rather, it is a reflection of the author's personal experiences and insights, shared with the hope that they may be helpful to others on their own professional journeys.

The certifications and learning paths discussed in this book are based on the author's own career and the resources that proved valuable in their development. However, each individual's journey in project management is unique, and the experiences shared here may not apply to everyone in the same way. While the advice and suggestions in this book are meant to offer direction, they are by no means a one-size-fits-all solution.

Project management is a dynamic field, and the certifications, training programs, and resources that work best for you will depend on your personal goals, industry, and the specific challenges you face. The author's aim is simply to provide a glimpse into what has worked for them, with the understanding that other professionals may find different paths that suit their own needs.

Ultimately, this book serves as a guide grounded in personal experience, but it is not a blueprint for everyone. It is important to consider your own aspirations, research available options, and choose the learning and certification opportunities that align with your career objectives.

As you read, keep in mind that this is a personal perspective, and while the experiences and suggestions shared here may offer valuable insights, they are only part of the broader landscape of project management learning and development.

Contents

Introduction 1

Section1: The foundations of Leadership 3
1.1 From Techie to Manager 4
1.2. People Over Processes 8
1.3 The Emotional Compass 12

Section 2: Tales from Trenches 19
2.1 The Deadline That Refused to Budge 20
2.2 When the Plan Goes Off the Rails 26
2.3 Unsung Heroes of the Project World 30
2.4 Lessons Learned 36

Section 3: The Balancing Act 39
3.1 Managing the Managers 40
3.2 Work-Life, or Life-Work? 47
3.3 Celebrating the Small Wins 53

Section 4: Strategies of Survival 61
4.1 The Art of Saying No 62
4.2 Dealing with Difficult Personalities 68
4.3 From Chaos to Clarity 75

Section5: The Lighter Side of Deadlines 81
5.1 Project Management: A Comedy of Errors 82
5.2 Meetings That Could Have Been Emails 89

5.3 Deadlines Do not Define You.................................95

Bonus Section 100

Bonus 1.PM Survival Kit: Must-Have Tools, Skills, and Mindsets for Every Project Manager 101

Bonus 2. Letters to My Younger Self: Advice I'd Give to Myself When Starting My Career 104

Conclusion: "The Bigger Picture" 112

Introduction

Welcome to the world of project management—a world filled with constant change, unexpected challenges, and the thrill of turning chaos into order. In this book, we're not just talking about managing timelines, budgets, or tasks; we're diving deep into the human aspect of the job, where the true magic of leadership happens. Whether you're an experienced project manager or just starting your career, this book is designed to give you an honest, real-world perspective on what it's truly like to be at the helm of a project.

Think of this book as a collection of stories, insights, and lessons learned from the trenches of project management. It's not a technical manual or a step-by-step guide to certifications (though we'll touch on those, too)—this is about the messy, emotional, and often unpredictable side of the job. We'll explore everything from the transition from individual contributor to leader, to the art of managing difficult personalities and handling impossible deadlines.

Through the lens of personal experience, this book aims to provide practical strategies for success, reflections on the challenges we all face, and a few laughs along the way. From tales of failure that turned into invaluable lessons, to the humor that can be found even in the most chaotic of project environments, you'll find that the key to thriving as a project manager is not just about getting things done—it's about how you navigate the ups and downs of human interactions, balance competing priorities, and maintain your sanity in the process.

Ultimately, this book is a celebration of the people behind the projects. It's about the unsung heroes who make things happen and the importance of empathy, emotional intelligence, and leadership in driving a team to success. So, buckle up—project management is a wild ride, and this book will be your guide to not only surviving it, but thriving through it. Welcome to the Chaos Club!

Section 1:
The foundations of Leadership

Leadership is not about titles or authority; it's about inspiring trust, fostering collaboration, and driving a shared vision. Throughout my journey from a technologist to a project manager, I've learned that true leadership is rooted in empathy, adaptability, and resilience. It's about listening more than speaking, understanding diverse perspectives, and empowering teams to reach their full potential.

My experience has taught me that a leader's strength lies in balancing the needs of people with the demands of processes. Whether it's guiding a team through tight deadlines, resolving conflicts with stakeholders, or simply celebrating small wins, the essence of leadership is the ability to inspire and support others.

Leadership is not a one-size-fits-all skill—it evolves with every challenge, every team, and every project. It's a journey of continuous learning, where mistakes become lessons, and successes become milestones. To lead effectively, one must embrace change, value relationships, and never lose sight of the bigger picture.

1.1 From Techie to Manager

The transition from individual contributor to managing teams, with lessons learned along the way.

From Semester Crunch to Project Deadlines: The Engineer's Training Ground

When I reflect on my journey from being an engineer to becoming a project manager, I realize that my real training did not begin in the office. It started in the chaos of my engineering days, where deadlines were not just a part of life—they *were* life. Anyone who has been through engineering can relate to this: 4.5-month semesters packed with more tasks than should be humanly possible, a relentless parade of internal exams, assessments, and those dreaded words— *"complete all the chapters."*

The Art of Surviving Chaos

Back in those days, we did not talk about "task prioritization" or "time management." No, we had a simpler term for it: *survival.* Each semester began with grand intentions. I would organize my notes, plan my study schedule, and tell myself, "This time, I'm going to stay ahead of everything!" Of course, by the second month, that dream would crumble. The assignments would pile up, the deadlines would overlap, and the exam timetable would arrive like a ticking time bomb.

There were moments when I genuinely wondered if engineering was some sort of cosmic joke. How many subjects were there in a semester? Frankly, I lost count. It felt like 50, though I'm sure it was less—barely. But it was not just the number of subjects; it was the weight of expectations. Completing a syllabus that seemed endless in just a few weeks was nothing short of a miracle.

The Power of Confidence (and Creative Guesswork)

By the time exams rolled around, it was not about mastering the material—it was about *strategic decision-making.* As engineers, we perfected the art of figuring out which topics were most likely to appear in the exam. Call it intuition, call it statistical analysis, or just call it desperation—it worked. I would pick the most important chapters, skim them at lightning speed, and hope for the best.

Surprisingly, this strategy rarely failed. I'd sit for exams with confidence—not because I knew everything, but because I knew enough. And let us be honest, "enough" was the mantra of every engineering student. The goal was not perfection; it was about hitting that magical threshold that let you pass and live to fight another semester.

Lessons That Last a Lifetime

Looking back, those semesters taught me some invaluable lessons.

1. Prioritization Under Pressure: When you are staring at a syllabus the size of an encyclopaedia and have just a few days to prepare, you learn very quickly how to separate the "must-haves" from the "nice-to-haves."

2. The Importance of Focus: There is nothing quite like a looming deadline to sharpen your focus. Even the most distracted students learned to tune out the world and get things done—at least for a while.

3. Finding Humour in the Struggle: Perhaps the most important lesson was learning to laugh through the chaos. Whether it was a last-minute group study session or a shared panic over a difficult subject, those moments of camaraderie and humour kept us going.

From College to Corporate Deadlines

Fast forward to my professional life, and I have realized that the essence of those engineering semesters is the same as managing projects. The syllabus is now replaced by client expectations, the internal exams by stakeholder meetings, and the final exams by project deadlines. But the underlying skills—prioritization, focus, and humour—remain unchanged.

Even today, when faced with an impossible deadline, I think back to those engineering days. If I could survive a semester juggling assessments, exams, and endless chapters, I can surely handle a project timeline. After all, deadlines are not new to me—they're just old friends in new disguises.

A Tribute to the Engineer Within

So, to all my fellow engineers-turned-professionals, this section is for you. Let us admit it: our engineering days were chaotic, overwhelming, and often hilarious. But they were also the perfect training ground for the challenges we face today. Those semesters did not just prepare us for exams—they prepared us for life.

1.2. People Over Processes

Lessons from Life and Leadership

When I think about what it takes to achieve success, whether at home or in the office, one thing stands out clearly: it is the people who make all the difference. Processes, no matter how well-designed, can only succeed when the right people are in place to execute them. My journey as a working woman, a mother of two, and a professional with 18 years of experience has taught me that managing people is both an art and a necessity.

The Perfect Quality, Everywhere

As a mother, I have inherited the need for perfection and quality from my own mother. Whether it is planning quality family time or ensuring that my children grow up in an environment of care and positivity, I have always aimed to give my best. But achieving this does not happen without effort—it requires careful management of everyone around me.

From coordinating with the housemaid to ensuring the daycare staff is doing their part, to dealing with grocery delivery personnel, every task demands precise planning and people management. Money, of course, becomes a factor because delegating tasks and relying on others comes with a cost. But for me, the goal has always been clear: the process must be completed smoothly and efficiently, and this happens only when you enable and manage the people involved.

This experience from my personal life has shaped my belief that people are at the heart of any successful process. It is not about micromanaging or being overbearing; it is about creating an ecosystem where everyone feels valued and empowered to perform their role effectively.

The Office Parallels

When I step into my professional role, this same philosophy applies. Whether I am working on a project, leading a team, or managing change, I firmly believe that building a strong, motivated team comes first. Processes are essential, but processes Do not work on their own. They require a group of people who not only understand the steps but are emotionally invested in the outcome.

To create such a team, you need to focus on human connections. It is not just about assigning tasks and tracking progress—it is about understanding your team's strengths, challenges, and even their emotions. If your team feels supported and valued, they will deliver their best work. And more importantly, they will stick with you, even though the toughest deadlines.

I always say, "Log ache honge, to kaam acha hota jayega." (If the people are good, the work will progress effortlessly.) A well-managed team is like a well-tuned instrument; it does not just complete the process—it creates harmony.

The Human Touch: My Way of Working

Over the years, I have developed a way of working that prioritizes building relationships over rigid adherence to processes. For me, it is not enough to be professional—I believe in being approachable, empathetic, and understanding. It is this combination of professionalism and friendliness that creates magic.

When your team sees that you value them as people and not just as resources, they will go the extra mile for you. I have seen this time and again. When there is mutual trust and respect, your team will not hesitate to support you, even if it means waking up at 3 a.m. to help you meet a deadline.

It is not just about managing tasks—it is about managing emotions. If you can make people, feel like they are an integral part of the bigger picture, they will not only complete the process but will do so with enthusiasm and commitment. This is the true essence of people management: inspiring others to do their best, not because they must, but because they want to.

The Cherry on Top: Friendly Professionalism

Adding a layer of friendliness to professionalism is like putting a cherry on the cake. It is a fine balance, but when done right, it works wonders. Being friendly does not mean compromising on standards or discipline—it means creating an environment where people feel comfortable and motivated to collaborate.

At the end of the day, it is people who drive processes, not the other way around. Whether it is managing my household or leading a project at work, my focus is always on building a strong team. Because when people are happy, motivated, and aligned with your goals, success becomes a natural outcome.

The Lesson

Processes may define what needs to be done, but people define how it will be done. This philosophy has been my guiding light, both at home and in the office. By putting people first and processes second, I have learned that the journey becomes not just productive but also deeply fulfilling.

1.3 The Emotional Compass

Why empathy and emotional intelligence are the keys to great leadership.

Leadership is often described as the art of balancing emotions and logic. But when you are a project manager working against tight deadlines, this balance can feel like walking a tightrope without a safety net. I vividly remember a situation where my ability to manage emotions, relationships, and professional responsibilities was tested to the limit—a true test of leadership guided by emotional intelligence and a dash of humour.

The Challenge: A Skilled Resource and a Critical Deadline

Picture this: my team was working on a high-stakes project with a looming deadline. Among the team members, one individual stood out—a highly skilled expert in a critical area of the project. Finding him had been no less than a treasure hunt. Despite my efforts to have other team members learn from him, time and budget constraints had made knowledge transfer impossible. In short, he was the pillar holding up an entire section of the project.

And then, the unexpected happened. This indispensable team member faced a family emergency. With no backup in place, the clock ticking, and no room in the budget to hire a temporary resource, I was faced with the ultimate leadership conundrum. Do I:

1. Request an extension from the client, knowing full well this could lead to dissatisfaction?
2. Borrow a resource from another project, despite the logistical nightmare and potential backlash?
3. Tell the client outright, "Boss, this project is crossing the deadline. Deal with it"?

Or, do I find a way to navigate the situation with empathy, creativity, and mental agility?

The Immediate Response: Empathy First

In moments like these, empathy must take the lead. As a leader, you cannot and should not ignore the human side of the equation. When my team member shared their family emergency, my immediate response was, "Take care of your family first. We have got your back."

This was not just a gesture of kindness; it was a calculated decision rooted in emotional intelligence. Supporting my team member in their time of need was not just the right thing to do—it was an investment in trust and loyalty. People remember how you treat them during their toughest times, and this builds a foundation for long-term success.

The Mental Gymnastics: Finding Solutions Under Pressure

But let us be honest—empathy alone does not get the work done. As a project manager, I knew I had to think on my feet. Sitting back and sulking was not an option. So, what did I do?

1. Proposed a Revised Timeline:

The first step was to approach the client with complete transparency. Instead of focusing on the problem, I presented a solution. I explained the situation, proposed a realistic new timeline, and reassured them that this was a one-off situation.

- Humorous takeaway: It is like telling your client, "Aapka kaam zarur hoga, bas thoda patience rakhiye. Emergency toh kisi ke saath bhi ho sakti hai!"

2. Rethink Resource Allocation:

I analysed the tasks at hand to identify areas where the remaining team could step up. I reassigned responsibilities and focused on cross-functional collaboration.

- Pro tip: This is when you realize that every team member has hidden potential—they just need the right push.

3. Leverage Client Collaboration:

Sometimes, your client can be your biggest ally. I involved them in brainstorming ways to address the delay. This turned the problem into a shared challenge rather than a one-sided burden.

- Humorous insight: When your client becomes your brainstorming partner, it is like saying, *"Aapka project, aapki zimmedari bhi toh banti hai na?"*

Lessons Learned: The "Turup Ka Patta" of Emotional Intelligence

This was not the first time I'd faced such a situation, and it certainly won't be the last. Over the years, I have realized that these moments aren't about winning or losing—they're about creating a win-win scenario. Emergencies happen, and they're nobody's fault. What matters is how you handle them.

Here is what I have learned:
- Transparency is Key: Clients appreciate honesty more than you think. If you approach them with a problem and a potential solution, they are more likely to work with you than against you.
- Empathy Builds Bridges: By supporting my team member, I not only ensured their well-being but also earned their loyalty. This is a long-term investment that pays off in ways you cannot quantify.
- Flexibility is a Superpower: Processes and plans are essential, but flexibility is what keeps the ship afloat during storms.

The Final Takeaway

In leadership, you are often faced with situations where emotions and logic collide. The trick is to let empathy guide your actions while keeping a clear head to solve the problem. And yes, it is not always a smooth ride. As a PM, there are moments when you will think, *"Meri toh lag gayi!"* But those are the moments that define you as a leader.

So, the next time you face a similar challenge, remember:

- Empathy first, always.

- Mental agility and creativity can turn the toughest situations around.
- A little humour and optimism go a long way in keeping the team motivated.

Because at the end of the day, leadership is not about avoiding problems—it is about facing them with grace, grit, and a smile. And when you handle them well, even your toughest deadlines can become your biggest success stories.

Section 2:
Tales from Trenches

Project management is no less than a battlefield—full of tight deadlines, unexpected surprises, and countless moving parts. Over my years of experience, I've faced everything from last-minute scope changes to impossible stakeholder demands and the occasional humorous misunderstanding that could rival any sitcom.

Each challenge has been a lesson in resilience, creativity, and the art of staying calm under pressure. These tales from the trenches capture the essence of navigating chaos with a blend of strategy, humor, and unwavering determination. They're a testament to the fact that while the journey may be unpredictable, it's the stories, learnings, and connections along the way that truly matter.

2.1 The Deadline That Refused to Budge

A humorous account of dealing with impossible deadlines

Deadlines and projects are like inseparable partners—they always show up together, whether you like it or not. Throughout my career, I have handled countless projects, each with its own quirks and challenges. Over time, I realized that the more critical the project, the higher the likelihood that I would be assigned to handle it. It is almost as if my name became synonymous with "critical project handler."

In the early years of my career, I was part of the Centre of Excellence team, and my department was QA. The role equipped me with the ability to manage tough situations effectively. You could say I was "hardened" by fire—tough deadlines, high client expectations, and complex deliverables were all part of my daily routine. But one thing became clear to me: the nature of deadlines changes drastically depending on when you step into the project.

Starting at the Beginning vs. Jumping Midway

If you have been part of a project from the beginning, your strategy is completely different. It is like raising a child from birth—you know the behaviour, the quirks, the strengths, and the weaknesses inside out. With time, you develop a knack for handling the tricky bits with ease. Projects, like kids, may have their "tantrums," but they are manageable when you've been there from day one.

Now, the real challenge begins when you are asked to join a project midway and that too with a hard, non-negotiable deadline. Imagine being introduced to a child who has been spoiled for years—you Do not know what to expect. Will you get the calm, obedient kind (highly unlikely), or the pampered, mischievous troublemaker? Spoiler alert: it is almost always the second type.

The American Banking Client: A Case Study

Let me take you back to 2022, when I was chosen to lead a project for one of the most rigid American banking clients I had ever worked with. Here is the thing about this client: they were *very* different when it came to what they said versus what they did. Conversations with their upper management felt like poetry—full of promises and idealistic visions. But when it came to their written requirements or real-world expectations, it was like being thrown into a completely different reality.

When I joined the project, the timeline was already set—not by the operations or delivery teams but by the marketing team. Let that sink in. A team that is supposed to sell the product had created the project timeline without consulting anyone involved in the actual execution. Their promises to the client ignored critical details like constraints, resource availability, and operational complexities.

To make matters worse, the budget for the project was already tight, and the hiring process hadn't even started. It felt like being asked to cook a gourmet meal without any ingredients while being told, "Oh, and the guests are arriving in two hours."

The Realities of an Impossible Deadline

Here is what I was up against:

- Understanding the Project and Processes: I had to dive headfirst into a complex banking project, which involved learning not just the technicalities but also the client's unique way of working.

- Rigid Deadlines: The client was completely inflexible about the timeline. Extensions were not an option.

• Hiring the Right Team: With a limited budget and a ticking clock, I needed to build a team that had the exact skill set required for the project.

• Managing Stakeholder Expectations: The client expected flawless execution, while the internal teams were still figuring out how to get started.

The Humour in Chaos

Looking back, the situation was so absurd that I cannot help but laugh about it now. At the time, it felt like being thrown into a Bollywood action movie—dramatic, unpredictable, and full of twists.

For instance, I vividly remember a meeting where the marketing team assured the client, "We've got everything under control!" Meanwhile, my operations team and I were silently panicking, exchanging *"What are they even talking about?"* glances.

The real kicker came when I had to break the news to the marketing team:

"You have promised a Rolls-Royce, but we barely have the budget for a bicycle. So, either we redefine expectations, or we pull off a miracle."

Lessons Learned from the Unmovable Deadline

1. Adaptability is Key:

In such situations, flexibility and quick thinking are your best friends. You have to learn to adapt to whatever is thrown at you, whether it is mismatched timelines, limited resources, or overly ambitious stakeholders.

2. Stakeholder Communication is Crucial:

Transparency with both internal and external stakeholders is non-negotiable. When I laid out the ground realities to the client (politely but firmly), it paved the way for more realistic expectations moving forward.

3. The Importance of Teamwork:

Building the right team under pressure is a skill I honed during this project. It is not just about hiring talented individuals—it is about finding people who can work cohesively under tough circumstances.

4. Humour is a Survival Tool:

If you can laugh about the chaos, it becomes a lot easier to deal with. Even during the most stressful times, sharing a light-hearted moment with the team can boost morale and make the impossible seem possible.

Final Thoughts

Deadlines that refuse to budge are every project manager's worst nightmare. But they also teach us some of the most valuable lessons about leadership, adaptability, and perseverance. The key is to tackle them with a mix of strategy, empathy, and a sense of humour.

So, the next time you face a deadline that seems impossible, just remember: even the toughest projects can be conquered if you approach them with the right mindset—and a little bit of laughter along the way.

Because, at the end of the day, deadlines Do not move, but great leaders find a way to move everything else around them.

2.2 When the Plan Goes Off the Rails

Stories of unforeseen crises and how to navigate them

In the world of project management, no matter how much you plan, organize, or foresee potential risks, there is one universal truth: not all projects go as smoothly as expected. In fact, research and experience suggest that more than 50% of projects fail in some capacity due to various reasons—unforeseen crises, unrealistic expectations, changing requirements, or even sheer bad luck.

But does failure mean the end? Absolutely not. As a project manager, you are expected to keep trying until the very last minute. Even if the project ultimately fails, the experience and lessons learned are invaluable. A "failed" project may still pave the way for new opportunities, better processes, and the confidence to tackle future challenges more effectively.

Failure in IT Projects: A Common Reality

In the IT industry, project failure is often not a result of lack of effort or expertise but rather a combination of factors that derail the original plan. These factors may vary widely:

- Shifting client expectations
- Miscommunication during requirements gathering
- Budget constraints
- Resource mismanagement
- Technological gaps

The important takeaway is that failure is not the opposite of success—it is a step toward success. Every failed project is a source of learning, an opportunity to reflect and refine processes, and a chance to grow as a professional and a team.

Case Study: Navigating a Cybersecurity Project for a European Healthcare Client

One of the most vivid examples of a plan going off the rails comes from my recent experience managing a cybersecurity project for a European healthcare client. This client was confident in their processes but significantly behind in adopting new technologies.

When I joined the project, the groundwork had already been laid by another project manager:

- Requirements had been gathered and articulated.
- Budget and resource allocations were in place.
- Client approvals and sign-offs had been secured.

It seemed like the perfect setup—a dream project, right? But as they say, *the devil is in the details*.

The Challenges That Surfaced

1. Changing Expectations During Demonstrations:

As we started delivering milestones and demonstrating the progress, the client began to introduce new expectations. These changes were often subtle at first—an additional feature here, a slight adjustment there. By the third round of demonstrations, the requirements had morphed into something entirely different from what was originally agreed upon.

2. Rigid and Harsh Client Responses:

Despite explaining the impact of these changes on the budget and timeline, the client was rigid in their expectations. They were unwilling to compromise, yet they demanded that the project be delivered on the original timeline and budget.

3. Communication Gaps:

Despite the increased frequency of communication, there were clear gaps in mutual understanding. The client's vision for the project had evolved, but this was not communicated effectively until it was too late.

The Tough Decision

Eventually, the situation reached a breaking point. We were left with two options:

- Proceed with the current scope, knowing the client would likely reject it due to unmet expectations.

- Propose a new timeline and budget based on the client's revised expectations.

After thorough discussions, we decided to request a new timeline and budget. However, this decision came with harsh consequences. The client was dissatisfied, and the project officially went off track. While this was a challenging moment, it was also an opportunity for reflection and growth.

2.3 Unsung Heroes of the Project World

A tribute to the team members who quietly make miracles happen.

Unsung Heroes of the Project World

A Tribute to Those Who Quietly Make Miracles Happen

In the bustling world of project management, success often shines on a select few—managers, leads, or those at the forefront. However, behind every milestone, there is a group of individuals who consistently contribute to the project's progress without seeking recognition. These *unsung heroes* are the technical experts, support staff, and everyday contributors who quietly shoulder the burden of complex challenges, ensuring that the team moves forward.

This article is a reflection on their invaluable contributions and a call to recognize their efforts with respect, appreciation, and empathy.

The Challenge of Work-Centric Environments

In many organizations, the focus is overwhelmingly on *work, work, and more work*. Managers often drive results with a relentless pace, overlooking the need for appreciation and human connection. Unfortunately, this approach neglects the fundamental truth: employees thrive when their efforts are acknowledged, and they feel respected.

Reflecting on my own experiences, I recall a difficult moment after returning to work post-maternity leave. Instead of being met with support or understanding, I was told, *"You need to work harder now—look at others managing their work-life balance better!"* It was demotivating and disheartening, leaving me to question the humanity in such professional interactions.

What would have made a difference? A simple reassurance: *"We are here for you. Let us know how we can support you professionally and personally."*This is a small gesture but one that fosters loyalty, trust, and motivation.

In many industries, including IT and project management, resources are treated as mere numbers—tangible or intangible—who are expected to deliver results and then move on. However, recognizing individuals beyond their contributions is essential for building meaningful relationships and ensuring long-term success.

The Nature of Unsung Heroes

Unsung heroes are the team members who go beyond expectations, often working tirelessly to resolve challenges without drawing attention to themselves. They may be technical experts debugging critical issues, coordinators stepping in during crises, or even a peer providing moral support during tight deadlines.

For example:

- In a critical project phase, a senior developer identified a complex bug that threatened the timeline. Working late hours for days, they not only fixed the issue but also streamlined processes to prevent future occurrences. While the project lead presented a successful completion report to stakeholders, the developer's contributions went unnoticed.

- Similarly, consider a junior team member who silently takes on additional responsibilities to ensure the project meets its goals, often stepping into roles they were never assigned. Their efforts may not be highlighted, but their impact is deeply felt by the team.

These individuals often blend into the background once the work is done, much like passengers departing from a train at different stations. Their contributions remain etched in the project's success, yet they are rarely celebrated.

The Power of Appreciation and Respect

A small token of appreciation or a kind word of acknowledgment can leave a lasting impression on an individual. Unlike monetary rewards or formal recognition, which are often limited, genuine respect and timely acknowledgment create a lasting bond between leaders and team members.

Simple practices such as:

- Saying *"Thank you for your hard work"* during team meetings,
- Sending a personalized note of appreciation, or
- Publicly acknowledging someone's efforts in front of peers

…can boost morale significantly. These acts not only motivate the individual but also inspire others to put in their best efforts.

Fostering a Culture of Empathy and Recognition

As a project leader, I have always believed in acknowledging hard work and maintaining strong relationships. Here are a few principles that can help create a supportive environment:

1. Timely Appreciation: Recognize efforts when they happen; Do not wait for formal reviews.

2. Empathy First: Understand that team members are humans first, professionals second. Treat them with respect, especially during personal challenges.

3. Celebrate Milestones: Whether big or small, celebrate accomplishments as a team.

4. Build Relationships: View colleagues as partners, not just resources. Invest in their growth and well-being.

A Call to Action: Recognizing Unsung Heroes

The success of a project is never the result of one individual. It is a collective effort where everyone plays a crucial role. As leaders, peers, and teammates, we must ensure that no contribution goes unnoticed.

To the *unsung heroes* of every project—thank you. Your dedication, hard work, and quiet determination make miracles happen. You may not always receive the spotlight, but your efforts are the foundation upon which success is built.

Let us take a moment today to appreciate those around us who silently carry the weight of our projects. Because in doing so, we not only honour their work but also create a culture where everyone feels valued, respected, and motivated to give their best.

This tribute is a reminder that acknowledgment and kindness are not just professional courtesies—they are the cornerstones of a thriving team. After all, a small gesture of respect can leave a lifelong impact.

2.4 Lessons Learned

Both the client and our team took away valuable lessons from this experience:

For the Client:

- Clear Communication is Key: It is essential to communicate evolving expectations early and often.

- Respect the Process: Trusting the process and acknowledging the constraints of time and resources can lead to better outcomes.

- Be Realistic: Unrealistic deadlines and budgets only hurt both parties in the long run.

For Our Team:

- Document Everything: Having clear, written records of agreed-upon requirements can help manage scope creep.

- Set Boundaries: It is important to respectfully push back when client demands become unreasonable.

- Adaptability: Being flexible and finding creative solutions in challenging situations is a critical skill for any project manager.

- Client Education: Educate clients about the implications of changes on timelines and budgets right from the start.

Final Thoughts

In a service-based industry, the client is often treated as a "god." However, even gods can sometimes create chaos, whether intentionally or unintentionally. This particular experience was a perfect example of how unforeseen crises can derail even the most well-planned projects.

The key is to approach such situations with a problem-solving mindset, rather than a defeatist attitude. Yes, the plan may go off the rails, but every derailment offers an opportunity to learn, grow, and improve.

In the end, a failed project does not define your career or your capabilities. How you handle the crisis, extract lessons from the experience, and apply those lessons to future projects is what truly matters. Remember, even in failure, there is success waiting to be uncovered.

Section 3:
The Balancing Act

Managing stakeholders, upper management, and clients is an art of balancing expectations, communication, and trust. In my experience, it requires the patience to listen, the clarity to articulate solutions, and the confidence to make tough decisions. It's about understanding their priorities while ensuring the project stays on track.

At times, you become a mediator, at others, a motivator, and sometimes even a diplomat. Whether it's resolving conflicts, presenting realistic timelines, or aligning diverse visions, the key lies in building relationships based on transparency and mutual respect. The balancing act is challenging but also rewarding—it's where true leadership is tested and honed.

3.1 Managing the Managers

Tips for handling stakeholders, upper management, and clients.

If project management were a movie, "Managing the Managers" would be the most entertaining part—full of drama, suspense, and sometimes even comedy. As a project manager, you are not just managing your team; you are juggling a complex web of relationships: stakeholders with their demands, clients with their deadlines, and upper management with their expectations.

The secret to surviving and thriving in this role? Patience, situational understanding, and confidence. Yes, a bit of humour helps too!

1. The Power of Patience

When dealing with stakeholders, clients, or upper management, patience is your best weapon. Everyone has their priorities, agendas, and expectations. You will often hear:

- "This needs to be delivered yesterday!"
- "Why is this taking so long?"
- "Cannot you just add this one tiny change?"

Let us face it—patience is easier preached than practiced. Picture this:

Example:

A client walks into a review meeting and says, "We want the product to be user-friendly, quick to load, highly secure, and oh, by the way, it should also make coffee." You smile on the outside while your brain screams, *"Is this a project or a miracle?"*

In such moments, patience becomes your superpower.

- Take a deep breath and listen.
- Acknowledge their needs: "That's an interesting idea. Let us discuss how we can prioritize it."
- Redirect the conversation to feasible solutions.

Patience does not mean nodding to everything—it means keeping calm while steering discussions in the right direction.

2. Understanding the Situation—The Art of Reading the Room

Every situation demands a different approach. As a project manager, your ability to understand the technicality, process, and people involved will decide your success. Stakeholders may be business-oriented, clients may lack technical knowledge, and upper management may just want results.

Example:

Imagine you are in a presentation with upper management. You start explaining technical issues, like "API integration failed due to a conflict in data parsing." You look up, and their expressions scream, *"Why am I hearing Greek?"*

Here is the key: Tailor your communication.

- Upper Management: Focus on impact, timelines, and solutions. Avoid jargon.
- Clients: Bridge the gap between business needs and technical work. Show empathy for their priorities.
- Stakeholders: Balance optimism with realism. They hate surprises.

A quick tip? Read the room like you'd read a weather forecast. If the air feels stormy, adjust your strategy before the lightning strikes.

3. Confidence: The Glue That Holds It All Together

Patience and understanding are vital, but without confidence, they crumble. Confidence is not arrogance; it is the belief that you can guide your team, communicate effectively, and find a way forward.

Here is a scenario most project managers will relate to:

Example:

Your team is halfway through a project, and a major issue arises. The client gets nervous. Stakeholders start questioning your plan. Upper management asks, "What's going on?"

At this moment, your confidence becomes the deciding factor. You calmly say:

- "Yes, we've hit a roadblock, but Here is how we're solving it."
- "We're prioritizing the critical issues and adjusting the timeline accordingly."

The minute you project confidence, the panic starts to subside. Why? Because people trust leaders who trust themselves.

The Balancing Act: Clients, Stakeholders, and Teams

Handling managers and stakeholders is like hosting a dinner party. Everyone comes with different tastes and expectations, and it is your job to keep everyone happy without burning the food.

Key Tips:

1. Set Clear Boundaries and Expectations

Do not be afraid to say "no" when necessary, but always provide alternatives. Example: "We cannot deliver this by Friday, but we can prioritize critical features and deliver those by Monday."

2. Communicate Early and Often

Stakeholders hate last-minute surprises. Keep them informed, even when things go wrong. It is better to say, "We're addressing the delay," than to say nothing and let panic set in.

3. Be the Bridge Between Teams and Management

Teams may not always understand stakeholder demands, and stakeholders may not grasp technical limitations. You are the translator.

4. Sprinkle Humour into Tense Situations

When a stakeholder demands the impossible, sometimes a little light-hearted humour can soften the blow. Example: "If I had a magic wand, I'd make it happen today, but since I Do not, let us come up with Plan B."

A Funny but True Learning

One day, a client asked me to "finish a six-month project in one month because their competitors were launching something similar." For a moment, I wanted to ask, *"Do you want me to build a product or a time machine?"*

Instead, I smiled and responded:

- "I understand the urgency. Let us focus on the MVP (minimum viable product) and prioritize the must-have features first."

The result? The client realized their expectations were unrealistic, and we delivered a streamlined product that still met their core needs.

The lesson here? Never lose your cool, no matter how unrealistic the request.

The Bottom Line

Managing stakeholders, upper management, and clients isn't about pleasing everyone. It is about balancing their expectations, understanding the situation, and handling it with confidence and patience.

Key Takeaways:

1. Patience is Key: Stay calm even when chaos strikes.

2. Understand the Dynamics: Tailor your approach to suit the audience.
3. Confidence Wins Trust: Believe in your process, and others will too.
4. Humour Helps: A smile and a witty response can diffuse even the tensest situations.

At the end of the day, managing the managers is about mastering the art of diplomacy. So, the next time a stakeholder throws an impossible demand your way, just smile and say:

"Let us make it happen—one step at a time."

3.2 Work-Life, or Life-Work?

Reflections on Balancing a Demanding Career with Family Life

Balancing a demanding career with family life is like walking a tightrope—except the tightrope is on fire, you are juggling flaming pins, and someone keeps throwing surprises at you. As a working mother, this balance feels less like a neatly divided schedule and more like a chaotic symphony, where somehow, everything comes together in the end (mostly).

Let me take you on a journey through this tightrope walk, with all its humorous, heartfelt, and hectic moments, while sharing the lessons I have learned along the way.

1. The Dual Role: Mother and Manager

At work, I'm the project manager. At home, I'm the CEO of Family Operations. Both roles demand strategic planning, problem-solving, and the ability to manage people. The main difference?

• At work, my team listens (mostly).

• At home, my kids often act like *"project blockers"* who refuse to cooperate unless bribed with chocolates.

Example:

One day, I was in the middle of an intense client call, negotiating a tight deadline. Suddenly, my younger son barged in, yelling, "Mom! The Wi-Fi isn't working, and I NEED IT NOW!" As I muted myself to address the "critical issue," I thought, *"This is just another escalation, except the stakeholder is five years old and does not care about my KPIs."*

The lesson? Flexibility is key. Whether it is a client or your child, both expect your immediate attention, and you have to prioritize without losing your cool.

2. Work-Life Boundaries: A Myth or a Reality?

In theory, there is a clear line between work and life. In reality, that line is blurred beyond recognition, especially in the world of hybrid work. Your office is your dining table, your colleagues are on Zoom, and your kids are your uninvited *meeting crashers.*

Example:

One day, during a critical presentation to upper management, my son appeared on camera wearing a cape and declared, "I am Superman! And Mom is my assistant!" Everyone burst into laughter, but I had to think quickly. I said, "Superman and I are working on saving the day—let us continue with the presentation."

The takeaway? Own the chaos. People appreciate authenticity, and a little humour can turn an awkward situation into a memorable moment.

3. The Invisible Job: Managing the Managers at Home

At home, managing my family feels a lot like managing stakeholders:

• My husband is the *"strategic partner"* who sometimes needs reminders about his deliverables (like grocery shopping).

• My kids are *"end users"* who want everything to be perfect but have no idea how much effort goes into making it happen.

Example:

One weekend, I planned a "perfect family day"—breakfast, park visit, and a movie night. But by mid-morning, my elder son declared the breakfast "boring," my younger son threw a tantrum over socks, and my husband forgot to charge the car. I thought, *"If this were a project, I'd fire half my team!"*

The lesson? Perfection is overrated. Sometimes, just getting through the day with everyone alive and (mostly) happy is a win.

4. The Power of Delegation: At Work and at Home

If there is one skill every project manager must master, it is delegation. But let use honest—it is harder to delegate at home. At work, I can assign tasks and expect results. At home, if I ask my kids to "clean up their toys," they somehow interpret it as "scatter them across every room."

Example:

One evening, I asked my husband to handle dinner because I had a late meeting. He proudly served instant noodles. The kids were thrilled, but I couldn't help but think, *"If only stakeholders were this easy to please."*

The takeaway? Lower your expectations (sometimes). Not everything has to be perfect. Focus on what truly matters and let the small stuff slide.

5. Time Management: The Holy Grail

Time management is the cornerstone of balancing work and life. But even the best-laid plans can fall apart when you are managing two jobs (office and home) simultaneously.

Example:

One morning, I scheduled a quick team stand-up call, thinking I'd finish before my kids woke up. But as luck would have it, they woke up early, hungry, and cranky. While discussing project milestones, I was simultaneously making pancakes, negotiating TV time, and pretending everything was under control.

The lesson? Multitasking is a myth. Instead, learn to time-slice: dedicate focused time to one task and then move to the next.

6. The Humour Advantage: Laugh or Cry? Choose Laugh

When things go wrong (and they will), humour is your best friend. It lightens the mood, reduces stress, and reminds you that no situation is permanent.

Example:

One Friday evening, after a long week, I realized I had forgotten about a school project due the next day. My son panicked, and I thought, *"This feels like a last-minute client escalation!"* We stayed up making a solar system model that looked more like an abstract art piece. In the morning, my son proudly presented it as "Mom's masterpiece."

The takeaway? Find joy in imperfection. These moments may be chaotic, but they're also the ones you will laugh about later.

Key Takeaways: Finding Balance in the Chaos

Balancing work and life aren't about achieving perfect harmony; it is about embracing the messiness and finding joy in the small victories. Here is what I have learned:

1. Prioritize Ruthlessly: Focus on what truly matters, both at work and at home.
2. Be Flexible: Plans will change, and that's okay. Adapt and move forward.
3. Communicate Clearly: Whether it is with your team or your family, set expectations early.
4. Celebrate Small Wins: Surviving a tough day is an achievement worth celebrating.

At the end of the day, it is not about work-life balance—it is about life-work harmony. Your career is part of your life, but your family is what gives it meaning. So, laugh at the chaos, cherish the moments, and remember: *You are doing better than you think.*

3.3 Celebrating the Small Wins

How Recognizing Milestones Motivates Teams and Keeps the Energy Alive

As a project manager, a wife, and a mother of two energetic boys, I have realized one universal truth—big achievements are rare, but small wins happen daily. The art lies in celebrating these small victories because they are the fuel that keeps the engine running, whether it is a work project, family life, or even getting your kids to eat vegetables.

Let us explore how recognizing milestones can transform chaos into celebration, motivate teams (and families), and keep spirits high—even when things aren't perfect.

1. Small Wins at Work: The Power of a "Good Job"

In the corporate world, celebrating milestones can mean the difference between a motivated team and a burnt-out one. I have learned that you Do not need a grand event to show appreciation—sometimes, a simple "well done" at the right moment is enough.

Story:

During a high-pressure project, my team was working late nights to meet a critical deadline. On a Friday evening, after we hit a key milestone, I ordered pizzas and sent a thank-you email to the entire team, calling out individual contributions. One team member replied, "This pizza tastes better than any award I have ever received!"

The lesson? Small gestures of appreciation, like pizza or a thoughtful email, can re-energize a team. They remind everyone that their efforts are noticed and valued.

Humour:

Of course, this led to the joke that our team's performance directly correlated to the type of pizza we ordered. When we ordered plain cheese, progress slowed, but a pepperoni pizza could work miracles!

2. Celebrating Wins at Home: Turning Chaos into Joy

At home, small wins are often overlooked, but they are the moments that keep families connected. As a mother, I have learned to celebrate every little milestone—even if it is just getting the kids to bed on time.

Story:

One evening, after a long day at work, I managed to convince my younger son to eat broccoli without a meltdown. I declared it a victory and made a big deal about it, saying, "You are now a superhero because superheroes eat their greens!" My son's chest puffed up with pride, and he even asked for more broccoli the next day.

The lesson? Celebrating small wins creates a ripple effect. It builds confidence and makes even the smallest tasks feel important.

Humour:

The downside? My elder son then demanded to know why eating chocolate didn't make him a superhero. I had to explain that superheroes needed to *balance* their diet—just like mom balances her work and life.

3. The Dual Role: Family and Team Celebrations

As a wife, mother, and project manager, I have mastered the art of celebrating wins in both professional and personal spheres—sometimes simultaneously.

Story:

Once, I was leading a challenging project that finally passed a critical phase. On the same day, my son won his first badminton match. To celebrate, I baked a cake for my family and took donuts to work the next day. While cutting the cake at home, my younger son asked, "Is this for my win or yours?" I smiled and said, "For both. Wins are sweeter when shared."

The lesson? Celebrating together strengthens bonds, whether it is with your team or your family. Sharing joy multiplies it.

Humour:

At work, however, the donuts sparked a debate about whether sweet treats should become a KPI for project milestones. Someone joked that the bigger the win, the bigger the dessert should be—a cheesecake for a successful launch, perhaps?

4. Small Wins as Building Blocks to Big Success

Small wins are like the bricks in a wall—they might seem insignificant on their own, but together, they create something solid and lasting.

Story:

In 2021, during a long-term project with a particularly demanding client, we struggled to meet weekly targets. Instead of focusing on the end goal, I started breaking the project into smaller milestones. Every time we achieved one, we celebrated with a team shoutout or a quick coffee break. By the time we completed the project, the client remarked, "It feels like this was a smooth journey." Little did they know about the small wins we celebrated along the way!

The lesson? Recognizing incremental progress boosts morale and makes big goals feel achievable.

Humour:

One team member joked, "If we celebrate this much for small wins, imagine the party for the final delivery!" I replied, "The final party might need a budget approval!"

5. The Joy of Acknowledgment: Beyond Work and Home

Recognition isn't just about achievements; it is about acknowledging effort, growth, and resilience. It applies to everyone, from team members who deliver on time to a toddler who learns to tie his shoes.

Story:

Recently, during a stressful project phase, I noticed one of my team members staying back late every day. While the deadline loomed, I decided to pause and thank them for their dedication. I wrote a personalized note and handed it over with a coffee voucher. Their response? "This means more to me than any bonus."

Similarly, at home, when my elder son tried to help his younger brother with homework (even though they ended up arguing), I acknowledged his effort with a hug and said, "You are such a great big brother!"

The lesson? Acknowledgment, even in small forms, creates a lasting impact. It shows that you care about the person behind the effort.

Key Takeaways: Why Celebrate the Small Wins?

1. Motivation Multiplier: Recognizing milestones keeps the energy alive and motivates everyone to keep pushing forward.//
2. Builds Positivity: Celebrations, no matter how small, create a positive atmosphere that fosters collaboration and resilience.

3. Strengthens Bonds: Sharing joy strengthens relationships, whether at work or home.
4. Adds Fun to the Journey: Let us face it—work and life can be stressful. A little celebration adds joy to the grind.

Closing Thought:

Whether it is a project milestone, a family achievement, or just surviving a chaotic day, celebrating small wins reminds us that progress is progress, no matter how tiny. So next time you face a mountain, do not forget to pause and enjoy the view from each small step you conquer. After all, life is too short to wait for the "big win." Celebrate today, laugh often, and keep going!

Section 4: Strategies of Survival

For anyone navigating the complex world of project management, dealing with stakeholders, upper management, and clients can feel like walking a tightrope. It's a high-pressure dance that demands a combination of strategic thinking, adaptability, and emotional intelligence.

From my experience, the key to survival lies in mastering clear and consistent communication. Always set realistic expectations, and don't hesitate to back your decisions with data. Be ready to adjust plans when needed, but never lose sight of the bigger picture. And when the tension rises, a touch of humor can be your secret weapon—it lightens the mood and reminds everyone that we're all in this together.

Remember, survival isn't just about meeting demands or checking boxes; it's about thriving in the chaos, building trust, and proving that even the toughest situations can be handled with confidence and composure.

4.1 The Art of Saying No

Setting Boundaries with Stakeholders and Staying Realistic

In the world of project management, saying "no" can feel like the riskiest move you will ever make. After all, stakeholders, clients, and upper management often expect miracles. But Here is the truth: if you Do not master the art of saying no, you risk overcommitting, burning out, and, ironically, failing to deliver. Over the years, I have learned that saying no isn't about confrontation—it is about negotiation, prioritization, and honesty. And trust me, with a bit of humour, you can even make it a skill worth bragging about.

1. The Fear of Saying No

The first time I had to say no to a client was like telling my kids they couldn't have dessert before dinner—it was terrifying. As a mother of two, I have mastered the art of firm but kind refusals at home, but in the professional world, it is a different ballgame.

Story:

Once, a stakeholder came to me with a request to "just add a small feature" to a project that was already on a tight deadline. I tried to politely explain the constraints, but they kept insisting. Finally, I said, "Sure, we can add it, but we'll have to extend the timeline and double the budget. Should I inform the finance team?" The stakeholder paused, smiled awkwardly, and replied, "Oh, maybe it is not that urgent after all."

Humour:

It felt like the time my younger son asked for a pet tiger, and I replied, "Of course, but you will have to feed it, bathe it, and explain to your brother why he's missing a leg." Both situations ended with a polite withdrawal of the request!

2. The Technique of Saying No Without Saying No

Saying no does not always require using the word "no." Sometimes, it is about offering alternatives or redirecting the conversation to a more feasible solution.

Example:

One of my clients once demanded a new module just two weeks before the final delivery. Instead of outright refusing, I said, "That's a great idea! How about we include it in Phase 2, so we can give it the attention it deserves?" They not only agreed but also complimented my "proactive approach."

Tip:

Turn "no" into a "yes, but…" For instance:

- "Yes, but we'll need additional resources."
- "Yes, but it might impact the existing timeline."

This way, you are not rejecting them; you are managing their expectations.

3. Setting Boundaries Early

One of the best ways to avoid saying no repeatedly is to set boundaries right from the start. Clearly define what's possible, what's not, and the trade-offs involved.

Story:

In one project, a stakeholder kept adding "just one more" requirement every week. It was like a never-ending buffet. I finally sat down with them and said, "Think of this project like a 3-course meal. If we keep adding dishes, we'll never finish eating." They laughed and agreed to stick to the original plan.

Humour:

It reminded me of family vacations where my husband suggests we visit "just one more" attraction, and before we know it, we've covered three cities in a day. Boundaries are as important in life as they are in projects!

4. Handling Difficult Stakeholders

Not all stakeholders take no for an answer. Some will push, escalate, or even try to guilt-trip you into saying yes. In such cases, staying calm and confident is key.

Example:

A particularly persistent stakeholder once said, "But this is critical for the project's success!" I responded, "I understand, and that's why we need to ensure we have the time and resources to do it right. Rushing it now could compromise the entire project." They grudgingly agreed, but it saved us from a potential disaster.

Humour:

It is like my elder son asking for permission to stay up late before exams, claiming it is "critical" for his preparation. My response? "Critical for whom? You or Netflix?"

5. The Power of Data and Facts

When emotions run high, facts become your best friend. Use data to support your reasoning and make the "no" feel less personal and more logical.

Example:

In a cybersecurity project, a client wanted a major design change mid-project. I presented them with a timeline showing the impact of their request on delivery and costs. Seeing the numbers made them reconsider without further debate.

Tip:

Let the data do the talking. A Gantt chart, cost analysis, or risk assessment can often say no for you without you uttering a word.

6. Celebrating the Wins in Saying No

Saying no isn't always about rejection—it is about protecting your team, your project, and your sanity. And when done right, it can lead to better outcomes for everyone involved.

Story:

Once, after a long discussion, a client finally thanked me for saying no. They realized that my refusal had saved the project from unnecessary risks. That day, I realized that saying no isn't just a skill—it is a service to everyone involved.

loved all the time—it is about making the tough calls when needed.

Key Takeaways from Saying No

1. Saying No is a Skill: It is not about denying requests; it is about managing expectations with clarity and professionalism.

2. Humour Helps: A light-hearted approach can ease tension and foster understanding.

3. Back Your No with Data: Facts and figures lend credibility to your decisions and help stakeholders see the bigger picture.

4. No is Not the End: Often, a well-communicated no paves the way for a stronger client-manager relationship.

Saying no isn't about creating friction; it is about maintaining balance and setting realistic boundaries. Whether it is a persistent client or a family member with a far-fetched request, the art of saying no is a valuable tool in every aspect of life. So, the next time someone asks for the impossible, remember: "No" isn't a negative—it is a step toward achieving what's truly possible.

4.2 Dealing with Difficult Personalities

Stories and Strategies for Navigating Challenging Team Dynamics

If you've ever worked with a team, you know that managing tasks is often the easy part. The real challenge lies in managing the people who come with diverse personalities, quirks, and egos. Over the years, I have learned that dealing with difficult personalities is less about "fixing" someone and more about understanding, adapting, and creating an environment where even the most challenging team members can thrive.

Here is a collection of lessons, real-life stories, and a few humorous moments from my journey as a project manager, mother, and, occasionally, unofficial team therapist.

1. Understanding the "Why" Behind Difficult Behaviour

Difficult personalities aren't always born; they're often shaped by circumstances. Stress, miscommunication, or even a lack of recognition can turn the calmest person into a challenging team member.

Example:

In one project, I had a senior developer who was brilliant at coding but terrible at collaboration. He avoided meetings, dismissed others' ideas, and worked in isolation. At first, it seemed like arrogance. But after a one-on-one conversation, I discovered he felt undervalued because his previous ideas were ignored in another project.

Solution:

I started involving him in brainstorming sessions, gave him ownership of key modules, and acknowledged his contributions publicly. Slowly, his attitude changed, and he became an active team player.

Lesson Learned:

Sometimes, all people need is acknowledgment and respect. Understanding their perspective can turn a "difficult" person into an ally.

Humour:

It reminded me of dealing with my elder son during exam time. His "difficult behaviour" often vanishes after a bowl of ice cream and some encouragement. Turns out, adults aren't too different—they just need a different flavour!

2. The Micromanager: When Too Much Involvement Hurts

One of the trickiest personalities to handle is the micromanager. Ironically, they often slow down progress by over-involvement.

Example:

During a cybersecurity project, a stakeholder insisted on reviewing every tiny detail, from font sizes in presentations to the placement of commas in emails. This constant interference created bottlenecks and frustrated the team.

Solution:

I introduced a structured communication plan:

- Weekly updates instead of daily interruptions.
- Summaries focusing on outcomes, not processes.
- A dedicated Q&A session to address their concerns.

This approach gave them a sense of control while allowing the team to work without constant disruptions.

Humour:

Dealing with a micromanager is like driving with someone who keeps saying, "Slow down! Speed up!

Turn here!" You eventually pull over and say, "Why Do not *you* drive?"

3. The Naysayer: The "It Won't Work" Expert

Every team has that one person who finds flaws in every idea and insists, "It is impossible." While their scepticism can be valuable, unchecked negativity can drain team morale.

Example:

In a healthcare IT project, we had a team member who objected to almost every solution proposed. "The system won't support it," or "The client won't agree to this," were his go-to responses.

Solution:

I reframed his role as the team's "Risk Assessor." Instead of outright dismissing his concerns, I asked him to provide alternative solutions whenever he raised a problem. This approach turned his negativity into constructive input.

Humour:

It felt like asking my younger son why he didn't want to eat vegetables. His response? "They're boring." My counter: "How about we turn them into funny faces on your plate?" Problem solved!

4. The Overconfident Star

High performers can sometimes be the most difficult to manage. Their confidence, while admirable, can occasionally border on arrogance.

Example:

In a banking project, I had a team member who believed he knew more than everyone else. He often bypassed processes and worked independently, which led to errors and missed deadlines.

Solution:

I assigned him a mentorship role, pairing him with a junior team member. This approach leveraged his confidence while subtly teaching him the importance of collaboration and accountability.

Lesson Learned:

Even the most challenging stars can shine brighter when they learn to work as part of a constellation.

Humour:

It was like teaching my husband that being a great cook does not mean he can use every dish in the kitchen without cleaning up afterward.

5. Strategies for Navigating Team Dynamics

While individual stories are unique, there are universal strategies that have worked for me:

1. Empathy First:

Always try to see things from the other person's perspective. Even the most difficult personalities are often motivated by genuine concerns or frustrations.

2. Set Clear Expectations:

Ambiguity breeds conflict. Clear goals, roles, and timelines minimize misunderstandings.

3. One-on-One Conversations:

Group settings can sometimes escalate tensions. Private discussions allow for honest, productive dialogue.

4. Celebrate Small Wins:

Recognizing achievements, no matter how small, can improve morale and motivate even the most difficult team members.

5. Humour as a Diffuser:

A well-timed joke or light-hearted comment can diffuse tension and make challenges seem more manageable.

Closing Thoughts

Managing difficult personalities is an art, not a science. It requires patience, creativity, and a willingness to adapt. Whether it is a sceptical stakeholder, an overconfident team member, or a stressed-out developer, the goal isn't to "fix" them but to create an environment where their strengths can shine and their challenges can be addressed.

Humour:

Remember, team dynamics are a lot like family dynamics. There is always someone who talks too much, someone who does too little, and someone who steals all the credit (usually the toddler). But at the end of the day, it is about working together to achieve a common goal—and maybe even having some fun along the way.

4.3 From Chaos to Clarity

Practical Tips for Staying Organized, Prioritizing Tasks, and Avoiding Burnout

When I look back at my 18-year journey from being a simple techie to a project manager juggling multiple priorities, deadlines, and expectations, one word summarizes the experience: *chaotic*. But as they say, every storm teaches you how to steer the ship better. Over the years, I have learned the art of transforming chaos into clarity—a skill that has saved not only my projects but also my sanity. Here are some tips and stories from my journey, sprinkled with humour because, honestly, what's life without a little laughter?

1. The "Inbox Tsunami" and the Power of Prioritization

Early in my career, I believed I could respond to every email, solve every problem, and complete every task on my plate. Reality hit me hard during my first major project. I logged in one morning to find over 300 unread emails—all marked "urgent." I panicked, replied to a few, and immediately realized I was just feeding the chaos.

Lesson Learned:

Not every email is urgent, not every task deserves your attention, and not every fire needs you as the firefighter. I started categorizing tasks into:

- Must-Do Now
- Can-Wait
- Why-Is-This-My-Problem?

This prioritization saved me from drowning in unnecessary work and taught me how to focus on what truly mattered.

Humour:

This strategy also came in handy at home. My elder son once came crying, saying his brother took his cookie. I told him it was not an urgent issue unless his brother ate the last piece of chocolate—then we'd have a real crisis!

2. Organizing the Chaos: From Post-Its to Productivity Tools

I used to live by sticky notes. My desk resembled a battlefield of coloured Post-its, each screaming for attention. One day, during a particularly stressful project, a gust of wind from the AC scattered my notes all over the office. It was a literal representation of the chaos in my head.

Solution:

I embraced productivity tools—calendars, task management apps, and good old spreadsheets. Tools like Trello and Jira became my best friends, helping me track tasks, assign responsibilities, and ensure nothing slipped through the cracks.

Humour:

At home, I attempted the same level of organization. I once used a Trello board to assign "tasks" to my family—laundry for my husband, homework for the kids, and "relaxation time" for myself. It worked for a week until my younger son "moved" all the cards to the "Completed" column to earn extra dessert!

3. The Time-Management Tightrope

As a project manager, time is your most valuable asset. But let us be honest, it is also the most elusive. I once had a client call scheduled for 6 p.m., a team update at 6:30 p.m., and my son's school play at 7 p.m. I thought I could manage it all, but as Murphy's Law would have it, the client call ran over, the team update was delayed, and I missed the first act of the play.

Lesson Learned:

You cannot do everything at once. Learn to delegate, set realistic expectations, and say no when necessary. Most importantly, plan buffer time for the unexpected.

Humour:

Now, I schedule meetings with a "buffer zone," which I call my "Oh-No Time." At home, I use the same logic—if dinner is at 7 p.m., I tell everyone it is at 6:30 p.m. That way, we actually eat by 7:15 p.m.!

4. Avoiding Burnout: The Secret Sauce

Burnout is the sneaky thief that shows up when you least expect it. In 2018, during a particularly intense project, I worked 12-hour days for two weeks straight. By the end of it, I felt like a zombie—physically present but mentally checked out.

What Helped:

1. Take Breaks Seriously:

Now, I schedule short breaks during my day. Even a 5-minute walk or a cup of tea can recharge your brain.

2. Celebrate Small Wins:

In that same project, I started celebrating even the tiniest victories—a successful demo, a resolved bug, or even just completing a meeting on time.

3. Set Boundaries:

No emails after 8 p.m., no meetings during lunch, and definitely no work during family vacations.

Humour:

My kids hold me accountable for this. If I'm caught checking my laptop during family time, my younger son yells, "Mom, are we your new project?"

5. Turning Chaos into Clarity: A Real-Life Example

In one of my most challenging projects, the client kept changing requirements, the team was overworked, and the deadline was looming. It felt like juggling flaming swords while riding a unicycle. But instead of panicking, I:

• Broke the project into smaller, manageable milestones.

• Conducted daily stand-ups to keep everyone aligned.

• Prioritized critical tasks and moved non-essentials to a later phase.

We delivered the project on time, and the client was thrilled. But the best part? My team came out of it stronger and more motivated.

Humour:

After the delivery, I joked with the client, "If you have another project like this, let me know in advance so I can schedule a vacation afterward!"

Closing Thoughts: Embrace the Chaos

Chaos is inevitable in both work and life. But with the right tools, mindset, and a touch of humour, you can navigate it gracefully. Remember:

- Prioritize what truly matters.
- Stay organized (even if it is just pretending to be).
- Take breaks and celebrate small wins.
- Learn to laugh at the absurdity of it all.

Final Humour:

If life as a project manager has taught me anything, it is that chaos isn't a problem—it is an opportunity to shine. After all, if I can handle stakeholders, deadlines, and my kids arguing over who gets the bigger slice of pizza, I can handle anything!

Section5:
The Lighter Side of Deadlines

Deadlines—those relentless markers of time—are often seen as the villains of project management. But if you step back and look closely, they bring their own brand of humor to the chaos. From last-minute curveballs to frantic late-night emails, every deadline carries a story that you'll laugh about later (though not always at the moment).

In my experience, deadlines have taught me the art of staying calm under pressure, improvising solutions, and finding joy in the most unexpected places. Whether it's a team rallying together in the eleventh hour or a client request that defies logic, there's always a lighter side if you know where to look.

For readers, remember this: deadlines might be demanding, but they also push us to discover our true potential—and provide plenty of stories worth sharing.

5.1 Project Management: A Comedy of Errors

Funny Anecdotes About Miscommunications, Mistakes, and Unexpected Surprises

In my 18-year journey as a project manager, I have learned that no amount of planning can completely prevent miscommunications, mistakes, or surprises. In fact, these little "errors" have often provided some of the funniest (and most humbling) moments of my career. Project management is, after all, not just about Gantt charts and timelines—it is a human endeavour filled with quirks, misunderstandings, and, let us admit, some outright hilarious situations.

Here is a collection of anecdotes and lessons from the field, where chaos became comedy and errors taught invaluable lessons.

1. The "Lost in Translation" Saga

It was 2015, and I was working with a global client. The client's requirements document was so detailed it could rival a novel. But the challenge? The document was in German, and while my team had some experience, none of us were fluent.

We decided to use translation software, assuming it would work like magic. Everything seemed fine until we hit a peculiar phrase: "Mundelein" (dog leash). The software had inserted this phrase in a section about data migration. Our puzzled team spent hours debating if the client wanted some sort of "security leash" for their data.

Finally, we asked the client for clarification, only to hear loud laughter on the other end. Turns out, it was an idiom that meant "keeping something under control."

Lesson Learned: Always clarify cultural nuances. And if a requirement does not make sense, ask. It is better to look silly once than to design a "data leash."

Humour Add-On: My team now jokes that we pioneered the concept of "data leashes" and that they could be our secret product someday.

2. The Miscommunication Memo

During a particularly intense project, I emailed the team, asking for a "code freeze" by Friday. Simple, right? Well, one of the newer team members, who was still getting used to industry jargon, took it literally.

Friday morning, he sent me a picture of a USB drive in his freezer with the caption:

"Code is frozen. What's next?"

I laughed so hard I spilled my coffee. To his credit, the team gave him the unofficial title of "Most Committed Developer."

Lesson Learned: Never assume everyone understands technical jargon. Sometimes, a little explanation goes a long way.

Humour Add-On: That developer still sends me pictures of his freezer whenever we talk about "freezing" anything in a project.

3. The Presentation Disaster

One of the most memorable moments of my career involved a client presentation. It was a big day, and my team and I had prepared a dazzling deck with animations, charts, and an inspirational closing slide that read, *"Together, We Achieve Excellence."*

As I clicked through the slides during the meeting, everything was going smoothly—until the closing slide. Instead of our tagline, the screen displayed: *"System Error: File Not Found."*

The client stared at me, confused, while I froze in panic. Then, our youngest team member quipped, "It is a metaphor for how we'll fix the gaps in your system!"

The room erupted in laughter, and the tension evaporated.

Lesson Learned: Always test your presentation on the actual device you will use. And sometimes, humour can save the day when technology fails you.

Humour Add-On: Now, whenever something goes wrong in a meeting, my team calls it a "System Error Moment."

4. The Case of the Missing Client

In 2018, we scheduled a critical meeting with an international client to finalize project milestones. Everyone was ready—my team, senior management, and even the coffee machine. But as the clock ticked past the meeting time, the client was nowhere to be found.

After multiple attempts to contact them, we received an email:

"We're ready for the meeting. Where are you all?"

Turns out, due to a time zone mix-up, the client had logged in six hours earlier. They waited patiently, thinking we were late, while we prepared for a meeting they thought had already happened.

Lesson Learned: Double-check time zones. Triple-check if necessary.

Humour Add-On: We now include "Time Zone Warrior" in our team awards for anyone who successfully schedules international meetings.

5. The Mystery of the Vanishing Requirements

In one project, we had meticulously documented all the requirements after multiple client meetings. Or so we thought. As the project progressed, the client suddenly started asking for features that weren't in the document.

When we pointed this out, they casually replied, "Oh, those were the *verbal* requirements. Didn't we mention them?"

Cue collective groans from the team. We had to scramble to accommodate the changes, but we learned an important lesson about documentation.

Lesson Learned: If it is not written down, it does not exist. Insist on documenting everything, even if it means being the "bad guy."

Humour Add-On: My team now jokes that we need to hire mind readers for future projects to catch all the "verbal requirements."

6. The Unexpected Office "Visitor"

Here is a lighter story. During a late-night sprint planning session, the office building's security alarm suddenly went off. Everyone froze. Was it a break-in? A power surge?

Turns out, it was a stray cat that had wandered into the building and triggered the motion sensors. We spent the next 30 minutes chasing the cat around the office, trying to "remove the intruder."

Lesson Learned: Always expect the unexpected, even in the most controlled environments.

Humour Add-On: That cat became our unofficial project mascot, and we named it "Scope Creep" because it showed up uninvited and disrupted everything!

Final Thoughts

Project management isn't just about delivering results—it is about navigating the unpredictable, embracing the absurd, and turning mistakes into opportunities for growth. Miscommunications, mistakes, and surprises are part of the journey, and if you can laugh at them, you've already won half the battle.

As a project manager, I have learned that humour isn't just a coping mechanism; it is a leadership skill. It helps build rapport with the team, eases tension, and makes even the toughest days bearable. So, the next time you face a comedy of errors in your project, take a deep breath, find the humour in the situation, and remember: every great project starts with a little chaos.

And if nothing else, at least you will have a funny story to tell later!

5.2 Meetings That Could Have Been Emails

Reflections on Unnecessary Meetings and How to Make Them Productive

If there is one universal truth in the corporate world, it is this: we've all sat through meetings that could have easily been emails. Whether it is an endless discussion about topics no one prepared for or a manager who loves the sound of their own voice, these unnecessary gatherings often feel like a slow drain on productivity. Over the years, I have encountered countless such meetings, and while they've occasionally provided entertainment, they've more often provided lessons on how *not* to run a meeting.

Here is a look back at some of my experiences and insights on transforming meetings into something actually worth attending.

The Marathon Meeting That Broke Us All

I once attended a meeting scheduled for an hour. That's already a long time, but we thought, *Sure, we'll cover everything and move on.* Four hours later, we were still debating the colour of the dashboard buttons in a software project.

The project's UI designer finally lost it and said, "If this meeting goes on any longer, the *buttons* won't matter, because the users will abandon the product before it is even launched!"

The room went silent, and we all agreed to move forward without further debate. The meeting ended, but not before everyone made a mental note to never sit through a meeting without an agenda again.

Lesson Learned: Never enter a meeting without a clear agenda and timeline. And if the topic can be resolved over Slack or an email chain, skip the meeting altogether.

The Status Update That Stole the Morning

As a project manager, I have often been pulled into meetings labelled "status updates." These meetings typically involve everyone reading off their weekly progress while others nod politely or stare at their laptops.

One memorable example was when a team member started detailing their work on a seemingly trivial task:

"I changed the colour palette for the logo design. It is now 20% more vibrant."

Before anyone could respond, the client chimed in, "Wait… we had a logo design task? I thought we finalized that last month!"

That one statement spiralled into a 45-minute debate, only for us to realize the task was assigned in error. We had just wasted an hour reviewing something that shouldn't have even been on the agenda.

Lesson Learned: Use a shared tracker or email for simple status updates. Meetings should be reserved for decision-making or problem-solving, not for narrating a to-do list.

Humour Add-On: After that day, we implemented a rule: status updates longer than two sentences would incur a "verbosity fine" in the team coffee fund.

The "Who's This Meeting For?" Mystery

Have you ever attended a meeting where it was not clear who the audience was? I once joined a session where half the attendees were developers and the other half were marketing folks.

The developers were discussing API integrations in painstaking detail, while the marketers sat there, visibly zoning out. At one point, a marketing executive interrupted and said, "This is fascinating, but I'm here to talk about the launch campaign, not… whatever 'API latency' is."

It turned out that the meeting invite had been sent to two completely unrelated teams by mistake. We all laughed, awkwardly apologized, and left feeling like we'd wasted a good chunk of our day.

Lesson Learned: Always ensure the right people are in the room. A meeting isn't a party—everyone does not need an invite.

Turning Meetings into Meaningful Discussions

Unnecessary meetings are frustrating, but they can be avoided with a few simple changes. Here is how I have managed to transform meetings into productive sessions:

1. Set Clear Objectives

Every meeting must have a clear purpose. Is it to brainstorm ideas, resolve a conflict, or finalize decisions? If there is no clear objective, it is likely a meeting you Do not need.

2. Use Agendas Like a Map

Distribute a detailed agenda in advance. One time, I forgot to send an agenda for a critical planning meeting, and chaos ensued. People came with wildly different assumptions, and we spent more time aligning on what we were supposed to discuss than actually solving the issue. Now, agendas are non-negotiable for me.

3. Timebox Everything

Timeboxing works wonders. A team member once asked, "Cannot we spend five more minutes discussing this?" To which I replied, "Five minutes leads to fifteen, and fifteen leads to infinity." It got a laugh, but the meeting wrapped up on time.

4. Embrace Asynchronous Communication

If something can be shared via email, a shared document, or a Slack thread, skip the meeting. Trust me, no one misses the meetings that never happen.

5. Call Out "Meeting Monsters"

Some people love to monopolize meetings. Once, a senior team member went off on a tangent about his weekend plans during a budget review meeting. I gently redirected the conversation by saying, "This sounds like a great topic for post-meeting coffee chats. Let us get back to the numbers."

The Joy of Cancelling a Meeting

One of the most satisfying parts of being a project manager is realizing a meeting isn't necessary—and cancelling it. It is like gifting everyone an hour of their life back. I once cancelled a weekly meeting after realizing we could achieve the same outcome through a shared task board.

The team's reaction? Pure joy. One person even emailed me, saying, "You are a hero. Can we nominate you for a workplace award?"

Humour Add-On: Now, whenever I cancel a meeting, I announce it with the subject line: "Breaking News: Freedom Granted!"

Final Thoughts

Meetings are a necessary evil in project management, but they Do not have to be painful. By focusing on clear objectives, keeping things concise, and knowing when to replace a meeting with an email, you can save time and sanity for everyone involved.

And remember, a good project manager isn't the one who schedules the most meetings—they're the one who knows which meetings are truly worth having. After all, in the world of work, sometimes less really is more.

5.3 Deadlines Do not Define You

A humorous yet insightful reminder that tHere is life beyond work

Deadlines. The very word can cause heart palpitations, sweaty palms, and an inexplicable urge to double-check your to-do list. In the world of project management, deadlines are as inevitable as Monday mornings and passive-aggressive emails. But if tHere is one thing my years of juggling projects, team dynamics, and personal life have taught me, it is this: deadlines Do not define you.

They may seem like the ultimate boss battle, but beyond the chaos of work, tHere is an entire life waiting—one filled with family, laughter, and moments you cannot afford to miss. Let me take you through some of my experiences, peppered with a healthy dose of humour, to explore why deadlines aren't the be-all and end-all of life.

The Day I Fought a Deadline and Lost (But Won Anyway)

Back in 2020, I was managing a critical banking project with an "immovable" deadline. The client, an extremely strict American bank, was as rigid about timelines as they were about their interest rates. I worked late nights, made endless phone calls, and skipped more family dinners than I care to admit.

Then, one Friday night, as I sat glued to my laptop, my younger son walked up to me holding a picture he'd drawn of our family. Only, in his drawing, I was replaced by my laptop.

"That's you, Mom!" he said cheerfully.

Ouch.

I realized at that moment that no deadline—no matter how important—was worth losing these precious moments with my family. I shut my laptop, declared the weekend off, and spent the next two days building LEGO castles and watching cartoons. Did the project suffer? Not really. We delivered on time, and I gained a renewed perspective on balancing work and life.

Lesson: Deadlines can wait, but your family moments won't.

The Deadline That Didn't Kill Me (But Tried Hard)

A few years ago, I was assigned a cybersecurity project with a European healthcare client. Their deadline was so tight, I joked that we'd need a time machine to make it happen. Despite my best efforts, the deadline seemed impossible, and the stress started taking its toll on me.

One day, during yet another late-night call, my husband decided to lighten the mood. He walked into my home office with a sign that read:

"Deadline Queen, but still human."

We both burst into laughter, and I realized how much I'd been letting work define me. Sure, the deadline mattered, but not at the cost of my sanity or the relationships I'd built outside of work. I communicated the challenges to the client, proposed a reasonable extension, and guess what? They agreed!

Lesson: Sometimes, all you need is a little humour and a willingness to push back.

Deadlines vs. Life: The Balancing Act

It is easy to get consumed by the urgency of deadlines, especially when you are leading teams and managing expectations. But Here is the thing: deadlines are just one part of your job—they Do not define your capabilities or your worth.

I have had projects that delivered late, and I have had projects that delivered early, but none of them mattered more than the time I spent with my family or the moments I dedicated to self-care.

Over the years, I have learned a few strategies for staying grounded:

1. Prioritize What Truly Matters

Not all deadlines are created equal. Sometimes, it is okay to renegotiate or re-prioritize tasks to maintain your sanity and personal life.

2. Learn to Say No

Every task or meeting does not deserve your immediate attention. Saying no to unnecessary commitments can save you from burnout.

3. Celebrate Life's Little Wins

Whether it is a successful project or your kid scoring a goal in their soccer match, celebrate every victory—big or small.

A Funny Reminder About Deadlines

I once had a colleague who treated deadlines like doomsday. He'd pace around the office muttering, "If we miss this deadline, the world will end."

One day, I asked him, "What happens if we Do not deliver on time?"

He paused, thought for a moment, and then sheepishly admitted, "Well... probably nothing catastrophic. Maybe just a slightly annoyed client."

And there it was—the reality checks we all needed. Deadlines are important, but they're rarely life-and-death situations.

Final Thoughts

Deadlines will always be a part of the professional world, but they Do not define who you are. You are more than your task lists, deliverables, and project plans. You are a parent, a partner, a friend, and an individual with a life outside of work.

So, the next time a deadline feels like it is closing in on you, take a step back. Breathe. Remember that even if the project does not go perfectly, you will still have people who love and value you for who you are, not for what you deliver.

Because at the end of the day, life isn't about meeting every deadline—it is about creating moments that truly matter.

Bonus Section

Bonus 1. PM Survival Kit: Must-Have Tools, Skills, and Mindsets for Every Project Manager

Being a project manager is like being a circus ringmaster, juggling deadlines, budgets, and team dynamics while keeping a smile on your face (and sometimes a cup of coffee in your hand). After 18 years of navigating the wild world of project management, I have compiled a "PM Survival Kit" that no project manager should leave the office without:

1. The Calendar of Destiny (or Google Calendar)

If you are not consulting your calendar every five minutes, are you even a project manager? The Calendar of Destiny is where all deadlines, milestones, and 3 a.m. panic attacks live. Pro Tip: Colour-code your calendar to differentiate between meetings that are "important" and "meetings that could have been emails."

2. The Multi-Tasking Superpower

Every PM must master this skill, but here is the catch: it is not really about doing 10 things at once, it is about pretending you can do 10 things at once while actually doing just 2 (and hoping no one notices). Sometimes juggling tasks means you are doing your best impersonation of a circus performer with a plate spinner.

3. The "No" Button

Learning to say "no" is an art. You cannot save the world (or complete every request). My tip: Always smile, nod, and say, "I'll get back to you on that," before running away as fast as possible. Bonus points for saying "no" with such grace that it sounds like you've just offered to solve world peace.

4. A Solid Sense of Humour

This is the most underrated tool in any PM's kit. When things go wrong (and they will), it is your sense of humour that keeps the team going. Whether it is a delayed delivery or an unexpected crisis, sometimes all you can do is laugh and hope your team does not see the sweat on your forehead.

5. The Power of Empathy

Project management isn't just about schedules—it is about people. Recognize that every team member has a life outside the office (even if it is a project you are passionate about). A little empathy goes a long way in keeping morale high and deadlines met.

Trust me, sometimes all a team needs is a "How are you doing?" to turn around a stressful week.

6. The Magic Wand (aka, Your Phone)

You cannot do anything without it. From Slack messages to urgent client emails to googling how to pronounce "scrum," your phone is your lifeline. Just make sure your "Do Not Disturb" function is on when you are hiding in the bathroom to avoid the latest crisis.

7. The Zen Mindset

No matter how many fires you put out, you need to maintain calm under pressure. I have found that a few deep breaths and channelling my inner monk helps. And if all else fails, try pretending you are on a beach in the Bahamas for 5 minutes during your lunch break. Works like a charm!

In conclusion, a PM's survival kit is all about keeping a balance between organizational tools, people skills, and a healthy dose of humour. With the right mindset, you will not only survive the chaos but thrive in it!

Bonus 2. Letters to My Younger Self: Advice I'd Give to Myself When Starting My Career

Dear Younger Me,

First of all, welcome to the wonderful world of project management! I know you are excited, a little nervous, and probably wondering how on earth you are going to manage deadlines, team dynamics, and clients who think "ASAP" means "five minutes ago." But do not worry, you will figure it out, and you will probably have a few breakdowns along the way (mostly related to coffee consumption and how many times you've had to reassign tasks because people suddenly get "busy").

Here is some advice I wish I had heard back then:

1. Be a Continuous Learner: Stay Ahead of the Market

You will constantly be faced with new challenges, emerging technologies, and ever-evolving project management methodologies. Don't let yourself fall behind. Stay curious, and make it a habit to learn. Whether it's through industry articles, online courses, or networking with other professionals, take the time to keep up with the latest trends in the project management space.

Also, don't just learn about the latest tools and techniques—try to understand the market dynamics too. By staying informed about industry shifts, customer needs, and competitors, you'll be better equipped to anticipate changes and position your projects for success. The more you know, the more proactive you'll be in addressing potential challenges before they arise.

Remember, the best project managers never stop learning. If you're not growing and adapting, you'll find yourself stuck in outdated processes, while others move ahead. Keep your growth mindset strong!

2. Be a Listener More Than a speaker

As a project manager, you will quickly learn that your ability to listen is far more valuable than your ability to speak. The more you listen to your team, your clients, and even your stakeholders, the better your decisions will be. People need to feel heard before they will trust you—and trust is the foundation of any successful project.

Take time to listen actively. Ask questions, seek feedback, and understand the concerns of those around you. Not only will this help you uncover potential problems before they arise, but it will also improve your relationships and allow you to make more informed decisions. As a project manager, you might think you need to have all the answers, but sometimes the best course of action is to ask the right questions and let others provide the answers.

It's okay to be a little less vocal when you're learning—your team will appreciate your willingness to listen more than your desire to be the loudest voice in the room.

3. Prioritize Your Mental Health

I cannot stress this enough: take care of yourself. In the chaos of managing projects, you may feel like your own well-being has to take a backseat. But trust me, if you don't take care of your mind and body, you won't be able to handle the demands of your job.

Set boundaries. Don't overwork yourself. Take breaks. Get enough sleep. Make time for activities that bring you joy and relaxation outside of work. A healthy, well-rested, and balanced version of yourself will make much better decisions and be more effective in leading your team. And when you have moments of stress or anxiety (because they'll come), reach out for support, whether it's from friends, family, or a professional. Your well-being is just as important as your project's success.

4. Expect the Unexpected (and Learn to Love Chaos)

In the beginning, you will want everything to be perfect. Deadlines? Check. Budget? Check. Deliverables? Double-check. But, spoiler alert: nothing ever goes according to plan. A vendor might back out, a key team member will unexpectedly leave for "personal reasons," and your client will email you at 11 p.m. asking for a new version of the product—yesterday.

So, embrace the chaos! Think of it as an exciting adventure where you do not always know where the next curveball is coming from. Sometimes, it feels like trying to juggle flaming swords while riding a unicycle—but hey, at least you are learning, right? You'll develop a sense of flexibility that will serve you well. The sooner you accept that things won't always go as planned, the quicker you'll adapt, and in the end, you'll find the surprises much more manageable.

5. Learn to Say "No" Without Feeling Like You've Ruined Someone's Life

You are going to get a lot of requests. Too many requests. Your inbox will overflow, and you will feel like the entire world is asking for something from you. Here is a key piece of advice: saying "no" isn't the end of the world. In fact, it is often the key to maintaining your sanity. Do not be afraid to set boundaries. You are not a superhero (I know, I know—disappointing, right?), and you cannot fix everything.

So, when your manager asks you to take on that impossible task at the last minute or your client wants you to change the project's entire scope in a day, just calmly smile and say, "I'll need to check with the team and adjust expectations accordingly." Then walk away with your head held high, even if you feel like crying inside. People will respect you more for managing expectations upfront than for overpromising and underdelivering.

6. Do Not Overestimate Your "People Skills" in the Beginning

Look, you are going to think that managing a project is about getting the most out of your team. Sure, it is, but managing people is a whole other beast. At first, you will be convinced that everyone has the same work ethic and mindset that you do. But, oh, the lessons you will learn.

The reality is that you will deal with people who want to do their best but are not as motivated or skilled as you think they are. There will be the perfectionists, the "I'm-too-busy-for-this" folks, and the people who just never seem to respond to an email (despite your best efforts). Your job will be figuring out how to work with all of them without losing your mind.

Remember: it is not a one-size-fits-all approach. Some team members need a little extra encouragement, while others just need a good push. And there will be times when you will want to "chat" with someone about their performance, but you will have to get creative and figure out how to do that without turning into a drill sergeant. Get to know your team members as individuals—their personalities, motivations, and working styles—and tailor your approach accordingly. This will make your job easier and will create a more harmonious team environment.

7. Do Not Forget to Celebrate the Small Wins

Young me, listen closely. You will be so focused on the big, shiny deadlines and final deliverables that you will forget to acknowledge the small victories along the way. Did someone on your team finally finish that presentation on time? Celebrate it! Did you manage to avoid a catastrophic deadline extension (for now)? Great job!

The little wins add up to a lot of momentum. Trust me, when you have successfully managed three crises in one day and you are still standing—do a little happy dance. Take a moment to appreciate what you have accomplished, because, spoiler alert, the next challenge is right around the corner. Taking time to acknowledge and appreciate small successes will help you stay motivated during the inevitable rough patches and remind you that you are making progress.

8. It Is Okay to Ask for Help (Really)

You are going to try to do it all yourself. You will convince yourself that if you just keep working harder, you can handle the workload without anyone's help. But it is important to recognize that asking for help is a sign of strength, not weakness. When you are feeling overwhelmed, reaching out to others can provide fresh perspectives, ease your workload, and ensure tasks are done more efficiently. Do not hesitate to delegate responsibilities or seek advice from colleagues, mentors, or teammates—they can offer valuable insights or take on tasks that may be consuming your time.

Trying to do everything yourself can lead to burnout, decreased productivity, and lower-quality results. By asking for help, you not only improve your own performance but also build a collaborative environment where everyone thrives. Remember, you are building a team, and one person cannot do everything alone.

Final Thoughts

Young me, the world of project management will be a challenging but incredibly rewarding journey. It will teach you lessons that go beyond deadlines and deliverables. It will shape you as a leader, a collaborator, and a problem-solver. Keep learning, stay flexible, and take care of yourself. You've got this.

With all the confidence in you, Your Future Self

Conclusion: "The Bigger Picture"

Being a project manager isn't just about timelines, deliverables, and budgets—it is about understanding the bigger picture. At its core, project management is about leading people, navigating challenges, and driving outcomes that impact both the business and the individuals involved. Over my 18 years in the industry, I have come to realize that while technical skills and processes are vital, it is the human side of work that truly defines success.

Leadership, as I have learned, isn't just about making decisions or managing tasks—it is about inspiring others, empowering your team, and showing empathy in the face of pressure. It is about recognizing that every deadline, every challenge, is an opportunity to grow, both personally and professionally.

What sets great leaders apart is the ability to see the bigger picture, to understand that every decision impacts not just the project, but the lives of the people involved. The ability to balance the needs of the project with the needs of the team, to push for success while understanding that people are the true driving force behind any successful project.

In the end, the human side of work—empathy, communication, understanding—will always be the ultimate key to success. It is what builds trust, strengthens relationships, and motivates teams to go above and beyond. As project managers, our ability to see the bigger picture and embrace the human side of work is what will ensure that we not only meet deadlines but create lasting, meaningful impacts.

www.ingramcontent.com/pod-product-compliance
Lightning Source LLC
LaVergne TN
LVHW061553070526
838199LV00077B/7022